The Miracle
A COLLECTION OF
INSPIRATIONAL POETRY

Nedra Anthony

Printed and Bound in the United States of America

Published and Distributed by:

Professional Publishing House

1425 W. Manchester Ave. Ste. B
Los Angeles, CA 90047

(323) 750-3592

drrosie@aol.com

www.professionalpublishinghouse.com

Cover layout: Richard Ike

Interior design: TWA Solutions.com

First printing, March 2012

ISBN: 978-0-9834444-9-7

Dedication

This book is dedicated to my daughter Juanita—the main reason I turned my life around. It was the only way I could help her when she needed me. Many of the poems are a reflection of our relationship.

Acknowledgments

A special thank you to my friends: Valrita Stallworth, Lottie Perkins R.N., Author, Bishop Bass Bullock, First Lady Adrienne Bullock, Linda Hudson Smith, Author, Helen C. Johnson, Author, Dr. Rosie Milligan, and Pastor Bennie Newton who went to be with the Lord in 1993. Without their encouragement, these poems might still be in the file cabinet.

Table of Contents

Foreword

$\mathscr{A}$s I edited these exceptionally inspiring and insightful poems, I felt deeply blessed and closer to God as each one of them ministered to me. It is indeed a privilege and a great joy to be able to help you share your marvelous gift with others, Nedra. Thank you, my dear friend, for this unique opportunity to be so thoroughly edified by your wonderful God-given talent. Undoubtedly, future readers will be bountifully blesed as well. Please publish your poems soon so I can buy and share them.

A Collection of
INSPIRATIONAL POETRY

No Clouds

Until I was introduced to Jesus
I did not know who He was
I did not have the slightest idea
He loves me like He does

Life is nothing like I thought
When I was a little girl
I found out I needed someone
To save me from the world

I started to read about Him
Learned of all that He had done
To give my life new meaning
Showing me who I could become

Soon changes started happening
Some I did not understand
But I was beginning to see
It was all a part of His plan

I work hard not to stray
In straying there is regret
When I did I found out
He is not finished with me yet

I know nothing will ever happen
That He has not allowed
And I keep on trusting Him
In my life will be no clouds

Nedra Anthony

All I Really Need

I have finally found
What I really need
I thank God for the wisdom
I know it is not weed
It is Jesus
He is all I really need

Since Jesus I have met
And to the devil's regret
I have found without a doubt
It is not a cigarette
It is Jesus
He is all I really need

Now I have heard my call
I am able to stand tall
I have found undeniably
It is not alcohol
It is Jesus
He is all I really need

One more thing I must proclaim
I caused my family a lot of pain
Now I am fully assured
It is not cocaine
It is Jesus
He is all I really need

But Lord, It's Tuesday

Thank you, Lord, today is Tuesday
It's coming up on eight o'clock
Now I can see part two of
My favorite show Matlock

What has he done for you
Can he fill your need
Go and get your Bible
Take this time to read

But what comes next I can't miss
My favorite actor wins the fight
I'll fix a snack before I watch
In the Heat of the Night

You said you would read at eight
And now it is after nine
I am waiting to bless you
When will you find the time

But Lord, it'll soon be ten
Right now I cannot bother
I promise I'll read your word
After I watch Midnight Caller

First you said at eight
Then you said at nine
A blessing is waiting for you
Are you going to make the time

Nedra Anthony

Okay, Lord, after the news
I'll lay here on the bed
My child, the news is off
But Lord, I am sleepy
I will read tomorrow instead

The Miracle

The Void

Before I came to Jesus
Many troubles had me bound
I invited Him into my life
And He turned my life around

He helped me see by trusting Him
My life would start to change
He said pray and do not worry
He gave me peace in exchange

He showed how much He loves me
I can trust Him by all means
He is the Master Builder
He built up my broken dreams

He taught me I am not a nothing
Showed me the something I could be
He already had His angels
Daily watching over me

Not just because He loves me
Do I want to do His will
Jesus Christ has filled a void in me
I thought no one could fill

Nedra Anthony

Another Hit

I once had a job
That paid me very well
If I were working today
I wouldn't be living in this hell

I took off my job
To give birth to my child
I was planning to go back, but
I would stay off for awhile

When my child turned one, I said
I will go back when she is two
I took one hit on a pipe
And bit off more than I could chew

Now it is harder than ever
To work will I ever go back
Because of a moment of weakness
I am hooked on crack

I tell myself that one day soon
I will go back to earning a check
I found myself selling myself
I had lost all self respect

For that reason my child suffers
I don't give her proper care
On the first my check comes
And I thank God its here

The Miracle

Rent is due no bills are paid
Seems I'm not worried a bit
I go and cash the check
Then go looking for a hit

I pay my bills from last month
And I only buy one rock
But, after that first hit
It seems I cannot stop

Now all the money is gone
My thoughts become real frantic
Then I think of rent and bills
That is when I panic

I start to wonder what happened to
The common sense I once had
Now I am depressed
Because I feel so bad

I am unable to see
The damage I have done
When I started smoking
It seemed like so much fun

Next month I will pay the rent
This time I am going to quit
Then thank God that on the first
I can get another hit

Sprung

Our children are suffering
For them we do not care
We put burdens on them
They should not have to bare

We have sold our souls
Our god's name is crack
We do not want to win
We are not fighting back

We lied and got on welfare
So we could buy a hit
We also sell our food stamps
We have no plans to quit

Anyone who tries to help us
That help we will reject
We have already given up
We have no self respect

We don't care about nobody
Not sorry for what we have done
All we want is another hit
Because we are totally sprung

The Miracle

Out of Me

My lack of prayer is one reason
My children are spiritually weak
Because of my mother's prayers
God's will today I seek

They do not trust in God
They chose to go the other way
Because back when they were babies
I did not teach them how to pray

Today they run with gangs
Have no fear of commiting a crime
Because while they were growing up
I gave them too little time

I pray someone will reach them
Before they end up in the grave
Now I pray every day
For their souls to be saved

Prayer is the only answer
He hears each prayer I've prayed
I pray He will let them live
For their souls the price is paid

I know that He will save them
If they seek to follow His plan
He saved me He will save them
He is the only one who can

Nedra Anthony

So! I will not cease to pray
Believing soon they will be free
Prayer is the priming water that draws
God's power out of me

Together In Prayer

Lord,
There is no one else to turn to
My life is all messed up
I come to you in Jesus' name
All I have is an empty cup

If anybody can help me
I know You are the one
I need someone to talk to
I am broken and undone

Something awful has happened
To one I love the most in this world
A man I let stay at my house
Raped my little girl

If I would have had a gun
I know he would be dead
I was passing her door
When I saw him in her bed

He knocked me down when he ran by
Lord, I don't know what to do
If I see him he is a dead man
That is why I came to You

I want to take my life back
Stop selling myself to score
These drugs have taken over
I can't live like this anymore

Nedra Anthony

If I let this rage consume me
I will never stop smoking dope
My child will suffer even more
And grow up without hope

My daughter heard me praying
I was still laying on the floor
She came over and prayed for me
Something I never saw her do before

She said,
Lord, you know how long
For my mother I have prayed
Asking you to show her
Some changes must be made

I hate how we have been living
But I love her just the same
Let her know that we forgive her
Help her overcome the shame

Now she knows the enemy
If she wants to change she can
Help her to decide right now
To do her best to seek your plan

We both know that You hear us
We place our lives in Your care
Here we are a mother and daughter
Agreeing together in prayer

The Welfare Office

People who come through these doors
Are of many nations, colors and creeds
Some are well educated
Others are unable to read

Some are here because
They have no education
Still others are here because
They have no motivation

Some are looking for a way
To support a deadly habit
Some want to feed their children
Who are hungry they can't bear it

Some are truly trying
To get back on their feet
Others have accepted a life
Of living on the street

Some are looking for a handout
Others are afraid to dream
Allowing problems to rob them
Of their self-esteem

Some once had a lot of money
Got caught in the devil's snare
While they lived a life of ease
Were never concerned with prayer

Nedra Anthony

Men, women and children
Come in by the scores
People of many walks of life
Had to walk through these doors

I could see how they were hurting
I saw it from their point of view
I can only write these words
Because I am down here, too

Stop and Give

Troubles put me in a position
I had to depend on the state
I went to apply for welfare
They said I had to wait

I was told to fill out forms
To fill out every sheet
I told them we were hungry
And we had no place to sleep

The questions were complicated
I needed help to figure them out
I prayed for them to help us
But my heart was full of doubt

I asked a lady sitting next to me
If she knew what to do
She said, I have my own problems
Why on earth should I help you

Then I began to cry
Tears streaming down my face
I felt so lonely and alone
With all these people in this place

I was laid off of my job
Then our lives hit the skids
This was the last thing I could try
To be able to feed my kids

We were put out on the street
All we owned was left behind
I looked for work from dawn to dusk
But a job I could not find

Finally, my name was called
I went to window ten
Picked up some more papers
I was told to wait again

With all my heart I was grateful
The next time they called my name
They gave us a check and food stamps
They gave us shelter from the rain

I kept looking until I found a job
I soon found a place to live
I know life is hard on the street
So now I will stop and give

A Beggar

One day I passed a beggar
Standing on the street
My heart went out to her
She looked so tired and beat

I searched for words to say
Where she is I could surely be
It is by the grace of God
That she is not me

I wanted to show compassion
Let her know that I did care
I did not have much money
What I had I wanted to share

I said, please let me help you
Let me buy you something to eat
She said, I hope you also noticed
There are no shoes on my feet

Without a second thought
We went to buy her shoes
She had a sweet and gentle spirit
No way could I refuse

Nedra Anthony

Kids moved away, her husband died
And left her all alone
She could not pay her mortgage
That is how she lost her home

She said, you look like you need help
I know just what I can do
I still trust Him you know
That is why He sent you

She grabbed my hands, bowed her head
Said, Lord, thank You for this day
My sister's heart is heavy
Please give me words to say

I hugged her and said thank you
What a pleasure it had been
Both of us were blessed
By the time she said amen

If I Were The Only One

Humble me, Lord, so I can't see
Myself for looking at You
Build on my mustard seed faith
I believe Your word is true

Make it my heart's desire
To follow the path You set
Teach me to obey and trust You
Not live a life filled with regret

Here are all of my burdens
I lay them down at Jesus' feet
I pick up my cross to follow Him
So higher heights I can reach

For when He died on the cross
Your every word He kept
Help me to have a mind like him
To gain that deeper depth

Help me to keep moving forward
With a daily supply of grace
I will come and meet You
In our secret quiet place

At first I did not understand
Why Jesus had to come
Now I know it was for me
As if I were the only one

Nedra Anthony

His Blood Paved The Way

God made a promise to Abraham
Said He would bless his seed
He would father many nations
All his descendants would be freed

Abraham believed His word
He would bless each generation
From that day a plan unfolded
The mystery of salvation

He and Sara well passed conception
But to God it did not matter
And when Isaac was born
Their hearts filled with laughter

Through Him the Christ would come
To die for mankind's sin
That was the only way
For man to be born again

Only those who believe in Him
Will ever be able to see
All the love that God displayed
By sending Jesus to set us free

God in His mighty power
Brought Him back from the grave
It was with the blood He shed
That the way was paved

It's Your Will

Lord, it is Your will
That my will obeys
And it is Your will
That lengthens my days

Lord, let everything I do
Let it be pleasing unto You
As Your will for my life
I pursue

Lord, it was Your son
Who gave His life for me
And it was His blood
That cleansed and set me free

I see how much You love
Your love was shown at Calvary
I want to serve You
With all You have given me

Please prepare me while I wait
For the day of Your return
Teach me every lesson
You have for me to learn

And, Lord, every day You give
By Your word help me live
Let it be Your will
That my will obeys

Nedra Anthony

The Miracle

When I started looking at life
From a different point of view
I found that I blamed others
For the wrong things that I do

Sin had a grip on my mind
So I did not understand
My life could be a better life
If I would take a stand

I was tired of the way I lived
Each day was filled with strife
At night I lived in misery
And nothing was going right

I had done so much bad
I could not recognize the good
Although I wanted to change
I did not believe I could

But God's love and mercy
Helped me change my mind
After I started looking I learned
He was there all the time

He removed the scales from my eyes
Which helped me clearly see
The miracle I was looking for
Turned out to be me

The Miracle

At First

Your life is a baseball diamond
You are standing at home plate
The choices that you make
Are what will seal your fate

First base is salvation
You must be born again
Believe Jesus died and rose
To cleanse you from your sin

After you pass first base
You must stay in the game
On the way to second base
You are trusting in Jesus' name

Passing second base you gain faith
His spirit comes to dwell inside
He will daily fill you up
you must let Him be your guide

He will help you understand
Your strength is in His word
There is still a long way to go
You must fight to get to third

Start sharing the good news
Telling why Jesus had to come
To pay a price we could not pay
The work has all been done

Nedra Anthony

He came and fulfilled the law
We are not under the curse
He is coming back to get us, but
We all must begin at first

At War

Jesus is the closest friend
I could ever hope to find
He saved me from myself
Then gave me back my mind

He wanted me to see
I could change the way I live
And there was no sin
He would not forgive

He said that I must trust Him
Told me He could fill my need
He filled me with His spirit
Told me to follow His lead

Let go of what is behind you
From Me nothing can you hide
Learn of the plan I have for you
In my word you must abide

He said it would not be easy
I had to watch the words I say
To always be slow to speak
And do not cease to pray

He said, if you fall don't worry
Confess it you will be alright
Don't trust in things that appear
You must never walk by sight

Nedra Anthony

Call on Me when all is well
Before a storm starts to roar
I will help you win the battle
The soul and spirit are at war

I Am Not Afraid

God knows more than me about me
He knows my every need
He knew that I would live in sin
With no desire to be freed

Yet He loved me anyway
On the cross He chose to die
When I learned that He loved me
All I could do was cry

I just simply asked Him
To give my heart relief
He took all my problems
And He gave me His peace

But! I must seek to find Him
Learn to follow His plan
Begin to share my blessings
With every one I can

He calmed all of my fears
He replaced them with His love
He is in constant prayer for me
In His home up above

I am assured I am redeemed
The full price has been paid
My heart is no longer troubled
And I am not afraid

A Breeze

I had to learn to place
My life into God's hands
So He could teach me how to live
According to His plan

Fleshly desires had me running
Until finally I got tired
Today, I run after Jesus
The flesh has now been fired

First, I was told I could fail
And sometimes I would fall
His spirit would remind me
On His name to call

Each day, if I resist the devil
From me he must flee
I have no need to fear him
It is he who should fear me

Jesus is with me every step
in storms I must go through
His spirit helps me understand
What He wants me to do

He teaches me to walk in freedom
To be the best that I can be
He helps me to stay focused
Not run wild because I am free

The Miracle

Living the life I am living
Has not been a life of ease
There have been some hard times
Other times have been a breeze

I Said

I said,
Lord, whatever I try to do
It seems I just can't win

He said,
There is only one way
You must confess your sin

I said,
Lord, it seems not to matter
Things still don't go my way

He said,
Do what I told you to
Get on your knees and pray

I said,
Lord, fill me with your spirit
So I can reach my goal

He said,
You must give your life to Me
Your heart your body and soul

I said,
Show me how to help others
And Your word to instill

The Miracle

He said,
How can you help others
When you don't obey my will

I said,
Lord, you know in Your will
Is where I want to stay

He said,
Then meditate in My word
Every night and day

I said,
Lord, what about the victories
I have already won

He said,
You can win them all
By trusting in My son

I said,
Amen

Still A Child

When a child is critized
They learn to condemn
Give them the love they need
By showing that love to them

If treated with hostility
They will learn to fight
They will grow up not caring
If what they do is wrong or right

The heart of a child understands
How Jesus must have felt
Those who wanted to kill Him
Were the ones He came to help

To the security of the father's love
A child will learn to cling
They know that they are loved
Joy to you is what they bring

If they are taught and encouraged
It will build their confidence
Show them how to walk in faith
And how to use their common sense

When a child is taught to pray
From the moment they learn to speak
They will grow up and the day will come
God's kingdom they will seek

The Miracle

God's love for them will keep them
As they learn to walk by faith
Walking in His goodness and mercy
Knowing He is a God of grace

They will know Jesus is the Savior
It might take them quite a while
After many years, I have learned
In Him I am still a child

Nedra Anthony

Child-Like Faith

I thought I could choose the way
I wanted to serve the Lord
Just when I thought all was well
I got caught off guard

I tried to do God's will my way
So I refused to wait
The trap was already set
And I went for the bait

I did what I should not do
I bit off more than I could chew
I did not consult with the Lord
Which I knew that I should do

I knew He would not approve
But I did it anyway
Now I am down on my knees
Searching for words to say

I wanted to live my life His way
But still trying to figure Him out
But I did not read His word
The reason I began to doubt

I wanted to learn to be humble
Learn to be meek instead of weak
To lean not to my understanding
To learn to think before I speak

The Miracle

I am learning more each day
About God's mercy and grace
I have learned in being His child
I must have that child-like faith

He Won't Turn

I started getting rid of habits
I thought I was too weak to quit
I put my will on the altar
To the Lord I did submit

I admited by myself I am weak
All strength comes from the Lord
By reading His word every day
I am reaping great reward

I was at the end of myself
That day I began to pray
Dear God, if You are really there
Please help me find the way

Show me which way to turn
I must stop running from myself
Only You can save me
I desperately need Your help

Then a peaceful calm came over me
I could feel God's love and grace
Something inside of me helped me see
There were facts I had to face

Jesus Christ really does love me
He gave me my measure of faith
If I believed and trusted Him
He would help me run life's race

The Miracle

He gave His life so I could know
God's every word is true
He is the only God you can serve
That will not turn on you

Nedra Anthony

According To His Will

I thank God for His love
He is gentle and He is kind
First, He got my attention
Then, He renewed my mind

Old things are passing away
Since I opened my heart's door
I have found real true love
Which I never knew before

He loved me so much
He died so I could live
He paid the price for my sin
Told me others to forgive

He laid down His life
God's Kingdom had to come
He returned to the Father
When all the work was done

We each have a measure of faith
On it He will help us build
Showing us how to daily live
According to His will

The Miracle

Make Him Smile

Through God's word I am learning
What it is He wants me to do
He makes it clearer every day
In Him I am brand new

He showed me the bondage I was in
I had no desire to be made free
That while I was running from Him
His angels watched over me

On the day I came to Jesus
He put my life on course
Soon I was filled with his spirit
Which is my power source

I had been a Sunday Christian
But through the rest of the week
I prayed very little if at all
God's will I did not seek

It took a whole lot of prayer
To forgive myself for my sin
Now I am on the road to being
The best me I have ever been

His command makes the world go around
His love makes the ride worth while
I want to live a life before Him
That will always make Him smile

Nedra Anthony

His Light

Through faith in the Son
The better I can see
Everything that He did
He did it just for me

The price was paid in full
The stone was rolled away
I could receive salvation
The Son has made the way

He is with me every day
He is changing the way I live
For I could never earn
What He would freely give

He gives me strength to carry on
When I am at my lowest low
Even if I turn and run
He will not let me go

He fills my cup when it is empty
Sometimes He fills it to the brim
He helps me want to do His will
As He draws me closer to Him

This is not an easy journey
Some days I have to fight
I learn to follow His lead
By walking in His light

Still

It took many years for me to learn
On my own I could not make it
Purpose in my life was unknown
But I thought I could fake it

After going down so many roads
I knew I should not take
I would pray for a way out
Hoping I would get a break

I mentioned all the trials I faced
How I got myself into this mess
I never would have done it if
I was not under so much stress

I doubted if I could overcome
Although the Bible says I can
Something inside said to me
For you God has got a plan

Every test you must face
Was nailed to Calvary's cross
His mercy and grace sustain you
When you are discouraged and tossed

The love of God is so rare
You find joy in doing His will
He knows your every thought
And He loves you still

Nedra Anthony

Off The Street

For years, I was addicted to drugs
Common sense had slipped away
With tears streaming down my face
I got on my knees to pray

I wanted to have just one night
One free from being high
My mouth moved, but no words came
All I could do was cry

I needed a whole lot of help
I didn't know what else to do
Seemed each time I opened my mouth
I bit off more than I could chew

I was losing a major battle
My heart wanted to win the fight
I was tired of chasing this thing
Which had taken over my life

From this life, I wanted to turn away
Wanted to start loving life again
I found out I could be saved
And be forgiven for my sin

The way had been made for me
Not to keep living in defeat
Jesus came into my life
He took me off the street

The Miracle

They Don't Have To Fall

You may be the only Jesus
That some will ever see
Your life is a living letter
To show others how to live free

There are many souls out there
Who have used up every excuse
Who want to turn their lives around
So put your time to good use

Many souls are ripe for harvest
And the Lord has chosen you
To show a lost soul His love
That is what He said to do

Many are out there searching
But don't know where to look
We can share with them
The words in God's holy book

Let them know that Jesus is there
Even if they should fall
He loves them so much
They don't have to fall at all

Nedra Anthony

I Don't Know

It really hurts my heart
Way down deep inside
To see a man abuse a woman
Thinking he's protecting his pride

He says, I love you, but
You really made me mad
She is wondering what happened to
The love she thought she had

He has no knowledge of love
All he wants to do is fight
After he vents his anger
He wants to have sex all night

She is afraid for her children
What if he takes her life
She has no family to turn to
None to go to for advice

The children are scared and worried
They, too, are living in fear
Begging, Mama let's just leave
Please, get us out of here

A decision must be made
She cannot take it anymore
She has to build up her nerve
To walk out of that door

The Miracle

Another fight is starting
Children are hiding in the room
She has got to do something
She must do it very soon

The fight is over; he is still high
He is passed out on the bed
She took his gun from his belt
She shot him in the head

Far too many women are abused
They don't know which way to go
Would I have done the same
I truly do not know

Nedra Anthony

Our Children

We must impress upon our children
And make them well aware
The world has no love for them
Does not have a heart to care

Minds destroyed by music and drugs
Soon they learn to steal and lie
Many of them want to get out
Think the only way is to die

They need a whole lot of love to
Get these thoughts out of their head
Some are killed some take their life
Too many keep ending up dead

Through prayer and working together
We help to lighten each other's load
Our children are paying a debt
That they never owed

Dear Daughter

A mother can be too helpful
Of her daughter she is so proud
The daughter calls it interference
Conversations can get quite loud

Some underlying resentment
Springs into the daughter's voice
The mother knew she had done her best
Not always making the right choice

The daughter:
Mama, you did me wrong
When I was a little girl
I am on drugs because of you
Trying to make it in this world

You try to correct your mistakes
By showering my daughter with love
Why didn't you love me that way
All my troubles you have caused

If you had been the kind of mother
That you should have been
I wouldn't have so many problems
Especially with these crazy men

Nedra Anthony

The mother:
My child, are you finished
I have needed to tell you this
If I could do it over again
I would only have one wish

For you to take responsibility
For the way you choose to live
My example was not the best
But my love I did give

Remember when I told you about
The day that you were born
I was close to death to give you life
Early on that Monday morn

I was sixteen years old
Only a child myself
Nevertheless, I am your mother
I find fault with no one else

You went home before I did
You had the best of care
Nine days later I came home
To a daughter with no hair

As you grew you developed
A great sense of pride
Now that you are a mother
You toss that pride aside

The Miracle

Whatever I did or did not do
I learned from each mistake
I taught you the best that I could
Hoped my mistakes you would not make

You did much better than I
You learned a trade and skill
Turn that knowledge into wisdom
Stop fighting your own will

You say that I have changed
The way I see it is growth
We can grow together, but
It will take effort from us both

This is not the time to grow apart
Let's grow together instead
We both want our baby to grow up
And know how to use her head

The bottom line is love
We cannot change the past
To be a mother or a daughter
Is not an easy task

Just The Same

We have had our problems
For sure, we have had our share
I know that God is with us
He has always been there

He created all daughters
I am one, you know
He chose me to be your mother
A very long time ago

He knows what we went through
He has always had a plan
For us to come together
And together we shall stand

Know whatever you do
In me for you there is no shame
Even if I don't approve
I will love you just the same

Up To You

If we keep on doing
What we have always done
We cannot expect any change
Few victories will be won

If we keep on thinking
The way we have always thought
We end up thinking wrong is right
In traps keep getting caught

If we want to we can change
Or grow with regret
What we have always gotten
Is what we always get

However,

We can change our actions
Stop doing the things we do
Only you can change your mind
It is all up to you

Younger Days

It seems you do not know me
You seem to think I do not care
I know there are times you thought
For you, I was not there

If I could I would go back
Live my life another way
I know what was missing
I never took time to pray

Forgive me for any wrong
You think I might have done
I know what I used to be
You know what I have become

I pray from this day forward
Together we will stand
Trusting God and each other
While we seek to find His plan

I had no confidence in myself
Did not feel I had much worth
Until the day I realized
God chose me to give you birth

I am amazed when I see
We are alike in so many ways
When I look at you I see me
In my younger days

The Miracle

First Rate

If little girls came in catalogues
Mothers could place an order
I do not doubt for a moment
I would pick you to be my daughter

I pray by now you know
You are very special to me
Although things are not the way
I had hoped that they would be

Through many trials you have learned
Life is not just fun and games
Both of us now realize
We need to make a major change

We must let go of the old
And grab hold to what's new
So we can clearly see
What God wants us to do

You are a very loving mother
As a daughter you are great
Know I will always love you
To me, you are first rate

Nedra Anthony

Go Find It

I had very low self-esteem
I knew that I was homely
I am a woman who sat waiting
Knowing one day it would find me

What I wanted would come
All I had to do was wait
I believed that it would find me
Before it was too late

One day, I sat and thought
It had to be coming soon
A long time I had waited
Twenty-five years come next June

Five more years I waited
Still it had not arrived
Fear had finally set in
I cannot count the tears I cried

I came to the conclusion
My thoughts were becoming clear
If I really want to find it
I would not find it sitting here

All those years I sat there
I wasted a lot of time
It was never coming to me
It I must go and find

The Consequence

Throughout life we search for
New expectations and new purpose
We look up we are in our sixties
We have barely scratched the surface

We spend our youth believing
We have a whole lot of time
We grow and learn and stop doing
All those things that come to mind

Some of us will come to ourselves
Stop playing the worldly games
Some of us will move ahead
While others will stay the same

The world owes us nothing
This should not be a total surprise
It is hard for some easy for others
To stop believing all of those lies

Our knowledge comes from the outside
Our wisdom must come from within
If we make right choices
We come out better in the end

We can choose what we want
It's best to use our common sense
For once we choose the circumstance
We must deal with the consequence

Nedra Anthony

Ammunition

I remember the day I realized
There was more to life than fun
I started feeling bad about
Some of the things that I had done

It was always someone else's fault
I would never blame myself
I constantly complained about
The hand I had been dealt

My mother never abused me
And my father was not there
All my life I had been given
Good advice and loving care

Self-centeredness played a big part
For others I had little concern
I found out the hard way
There were lessons I had to learn

When I met my first best friend
At eight years old I can recall
I saw her mom slam her head
Against her bedroom wall

It scared me so badly
I started running towards the door
I looked to see if she was coming
She was laid out on the floor

The Miracle

Some people cannot be trusted
With the children in their care
Today, I see much worse abuse
This is happening everywhere

I found weapons to fight for those
Who live in that same condition
Prayer, comfort and God's love
Is what I use for ammunition

Nedra Anthony

It Can Be Done

How can we claim we want respect
When we act like we are insane
We burned down our own neighborhood
Then said the white man was to blame

When will we open our eyes
So we can clearly see
We are in the shape we are in because
We are our own worst enemy

We think anything we do is right
Run around talking about we are cool
If we have so much sense
Why are we drowning in cocaine's pool

We gave our heritage to the white man
Gave our souls to booze and crack
We have all got to wake up
And start fighting back

Not by shooting and killing each other
We must fight back with a sound mind
But our minds will not solve the problem
If we stay high all the time

If we ever want to get the respect
That we should have always had
We must first respect ourselves
Being black is not that bad

The Miracle

A mother should teach her daughter
And a father should teach his son
Working together will not be easy
Helping each other it can be done

Nedra Anthony

The Praying Is Up To Us

There are a million stories in this city
All too many are never told
Some of us can see the pain
In the face of a hurting soul

One brother's mother told him
He was her biggest mistake
A father got in his daughter's bed
That father committed rape

Child abuse is running rampant
Like lambs being led to slaughter
Children are not safe in the home
With their own mother and father

Many parents are shackled in chains
Locked in the crack pipe's prison
Chasing after a high they cannot catch
Their kids make their own decisions

Some don't even put up a fight
Drugs are their only release
Weighted down with depression
They have no joy or peace

Some had goals they tried to reach
Low self worth kept them out of range
Wanting to live a different life
But did not believe they could change

The Miracle

The dealer says, I sell drugs because
There is plenty of money to make
The user says, I use drugs because
Nobody ever gave me a break

We must do all we can to reach them
Tell them in Christ Jesus they can trust
The Holy Spirit will do His job
But the praying is up to us

Nedra Anthony

Don't Make The Same Mistake

Make sure our children get knowledge
Teach them lessons to be learned
Encourage them as they are learning
For the young black men be concerned

Too many of them wear a frown
Seem to have nothing to smile about
Mad at themselves and the world
For how their lives turned out

They live a defeated life
Filled with troubles and woes
They count children they fathered
But do not buy them any clothes

Some are stripped of their manhood
Have very low self-esteem
Don't know what it means to be a man
Feel there is no need to dream

A man would be there for his children
Teaching his son to be a man
That with a good education
What he wants to be he can

The Miracle

A daughter needs a man as well
Without a father there is a void
That needs to be filled
Or that life might be destroyed

The mother is the only father
Many children have ever known
And the only reason is
There is no father in the home

A father and mother are needed
Of this there should be no doubt
Being in a gang can get people killed
They don't care whose child they take out

It has to be hard for these young men
Such a heavy burden they carry
They shoot and kill each other
Another brother they must bury

Prayer has changed some of them
Into a loving father
Some of them will give up
Soon they cease to bother

I was raised without my father
I missed the difference it could make
I speak to you young parents
Please don't make the same mistake

Nedra Anthony

Who's Going To Pay

I went to school in the fifties
I learned how to read and write
Mama helped with my home work
After dinner each night

I learned about our history
Slaves were freed, is a fact
Our forefathers lived as slaves
Because their skin was black

It was a crime to learn to read
Yet they clung to their heritage
Even when their children were sold
Still they were not discouraged

They fought and died to free us
We don't seem to want to be free
We shun a good education
We know nothing about our history

We don't help our children with homework
Some of our children carry a gun
Many people are living in fear
And nothing is being done

The school board keep having meetings
They had one just the other day
If we don't make some noise
Our children are going to pay

The Miracle

The Madness

We have come to a crossroad
Too many of us have failed to see
We have hurt the next generation
That is not how it should be

Many people died to make us free
Too many of us are slaves to crack
Too few of us are paying attention
Even fewer are fighting back

For a hit we will kill a brother
Leave him laying in the street
We let our children go hungry
They have to beg or steal to eat

It is hard to think if you are hungry
So what good is it to go to school
When we stay out all night long
For some reason we think it is cool

We will follow the rules of a gang
Then go shoot somebody's child
When the judge gives us natural life
We leave the courtroom with a smile

We have sold our children's toys
Stole from Mama so we could cop
Our children will grow up just like us
If this madness does not stop

Nedra Anthony

Our Pride

Our forefathers were brought here in chains
From far across the sea
That was over four hundred years ago
And still we are not free

They picked this country's cotton
From daybreak until dark
They were branded like cattle
Each wore the master's mark

And then a law was passed
It said that they were free
They had no money, no place to go
Still slaves they had to be

There was no welfare then
Too few of them ever got paid
Many worked until they died
And were buried in the grave

We are still slaves today
To one thing or another
We are armed with guns
Won't hesitate to shoot a brother

We are ashamed of being black
Something that cannot be denied
We gave away our heritage
Drugs and drink have stolen our pride

Black Pride

As a child I was called nigger
I had what we called unruly hair
There were those who laughed at me
Mama asked me why did I care

As a teen, I was a negro
Marched and prayed for the right
To be treated as an equal
I was light but was not white

In my twenties, I was black and proud
Thought that was a better way
To gain acceptance and respect
I grew prouder every day

When I was in my thirties
I just did my own thing
I lived life without purpose
Set no goals to attain

At forty, african american
Seaching to find out who I was
I had to prove to myself I am somebody
Began striving towards that cause

By the time I was in my fifties
I finally opened my eyes
After all I took myself through
God in His mercy let me survive

Nedra Anthony

Now in my sixties, I know Him better
Although I still have not arrived
The color of my skin has not changed
I now wear my blackness with pride

People Of Royalty

From our history we have learned
How we were treated was a disgrace
Those before us put it behind us
Still there are facts we have to face

The slave traders were successful
Filled our ancestors' hearts with fear
Minds were raped and babies were sold
And today we are still here

Living in those days was not easy
But they all knew how to pray
All they wanted was freedom
Some died trying to get away

Fact is, we must stand up
Stop shooting each other down
Start working together in unity
We need to cover a lot of ground

Fact is, we must get knowledge
As much as our minds will hold
Learn the difference between
Being ignorant and being bold

Stop letting the world rape our mind
If we believe we can learn
God has freely given us
The love we are trying to earn

Nedra Anthony

He has great love for all of us
In His word He has made it clear
A disciplined mind will help us see
There is nothing we need to fear

Teach our children our history
It will help them to realize
They can be as smart as anyone
Living under God's blue skies

We know growing up is not easy
If we live the day will come
Our minds must be our weapons
Not a twelve-guage or a gun

Take a look at the one in the mirror
Learn from your ancestors and your past
We can start being who we are
People of royalty color and class

Love

Love is like gold
Unrefined
You may walk pass it
Not knowing its value
You leave it

If it is polished
You pick it up
Look it over
And admire its beauty

Not wanting to be responsible
For something so precious
Some will walk away
Thinking they don't deserve it

Some receive it as a gift
And will cherish it
In the process
It makes life more fulfilled

Love is unique in its beauty
It outshines the purest gold
It is refined by the heart
And polished by the soul

Nedra Anthony

What He Wants

When Jesus knocked
At my heart's door
He gave me sense
To let Him in

I found out
How much He loves me
And
He died for all my sin

He said
I would grow in wisdom
And would learn
To walk by faith

He chose me
To be one of His
Told me my past
Had been erased

No strings are attached
To His love
He came
To make me free

He put the desire
In my heart
To be what
He wants me to be

If

If we meditate in God's word
Every day and night
We learn to use His power
Every time we have to fight

If we have His rod on one side
And His staff on the other
We have His Holy Spirit in us
Who helps us pray for our brother

If we have angels to watch over us
Keeping us from all harm
We have His peace within us
To make it through the storm

If goodness and mercy follow us
Everywhere we might go
We share His word with others
And they, too, begin to grow

If we all work together
To diminish the devil's flock
The love of Jesus will lead us
He is more solid than a rock

He will help us to help those
About to fall over a cliff
We can love them into His Kingdom
The key word here is *if*

Nedra Anthony

By His Spirit

I have wondered many times
How God could love me as He does
Why would He send His son
Without hesitation or pause

What is it about me
That His love would run so deep
Knowing all I have done
And my sins I would repeat

Then I was told He came to die
To bring me my salvation
If I would believe and trust Him
I could become a new creation

I prayed and asked for His help
I gave Him my every care
All went well for so long
I stopped going to Him in prayer

I even stopped confessing my sins
Until like a flood my troubles came
There was no doubt in my mind
Only myself could I blame

In Him I have the victory
In Him I have overcome
In Him I am able to see
The work is already done

The Miracle

Now my prayers are more consistant
I still have a long way to go
The more I study His word
The sooner my faith will grow

I thank Him all day, every day
For the love He has for me
Every day He draws me closer
By His spirit who lives in me

He Is

God is God before earth's
Foundation was ever laid
God is God when He died on the cross
He set the price that had to be paid

God is God when Eve was tempted
He is God who pronounced the curse
God is God when your life
Is at its very worst

God is God as Noah built the ark
He is God who sent the flood
God is God when Jesus prayed
And sweat great drops of blood

God is God when Daniel
Was in the lion's den
God is God when we believe
Jesus died to save us from sin

God the Son walked among us
It is He who made the way
For us to speak directly to God
Each and every time we pray

God is God the Holy Spirit
Who leads us to the truth
God who dwells within us
Making us fit for the Master's use

The Miracle

God is God always and forever
God when Jesus paid the price
God is God when we give our lives
As a living sacrifice

All creation belongs to God
Everything created is His
Seek Him and you will find
Almighty God He is

Trusting

By learning what God has said
Has improved the way I live
As I feed my spirit with His word
It bears the fruit that He gives

His mercy is everlasting
His love runs deeper than my fears
His grace is greater than failure
When I call on Him He hears

My children were little babies
When suddenly we had to move
I had to leave all I had behind
Or stay there and be abused

It seemed nothing I did was right
Made no difference how hard I tried
Not only was my mother sick
My very close friend had died

As the Greyhound bus pulled away
My kids asked me where is daddy at
We don't want to live with him
Mama, please don't take us back

I kissed them and said don't worry
Although I did not have a clue
I did not have much money
No idea what we would do

The Miracle

After my girls were asleep
My heart was filled with dispair
Someone handed me a Bible
Said your answer is in there

The answer:
I am never left alone
No matter what trials may come
Tomorrow will be a brighter day
If I am trusting in God's Son

Nedra Anthony

The Only Jesus

There are many souls out there
Who have used up every excuse
Not to trust in the Lord
Wanting to stop self abuse

Lives are filled with choices
Seeking to fill a void
Searching in the wrong places
Self-esteem is being destroyed

A life can change if we believe
That Jesus is God's Son
It is His love that draws us
The work has all been done

He came and paid the price
So those who believe in Him
Will receive eternal life
And no longer be condemned

When we tell someone about Him
When we point them to the tree
Remember
You may be the only Jesus
That some will ever see

Reap What You Sow

Learn how the devil works
In order to stop him in your life
He knows your every weakness
There is no weakness in Christ

He will put a thought in your mind
And if on that thought you act
You will suffer the consequence
He will not give you any slack

He will give you what you want
If it is not in the Father's will
He might even try to convince you
That it is alright to steal

At times we give him too much ground
When we listen to wrong advice
Best advice I have ever gotten
Was to give my life to Christ

He came into my life and freed me
His love changed the way I live
There is nothing I have ever done
That He will not forgive

I remember when I first believed
He would never leave me alone
I try to plant good seed in my life
For I will reap what I have sown

Nedra Anthony

Before It Fell

Being President of the United States
Is not the easiest person to be
Making decisions for a nation
Keeping all of its people free

Our history, if we know it
A thinking man can see
We have come a very long way
From where we used to be

We live in the greatest country
Fought hard to get this far
A lot of people lost their lives
To get us where we are

Some of us are still victims
There are more than just a few
They do not pay income tax
Their income comes from you

Victims keep looking for handouts
Waiting for forty acres and a mule
They say they want a better life
But don't have the sense to go to school

They will not go to the poll to vote
Then complain about how it went
The one who gets elected
Is the one that they resent

The Miracle

We fight a battle that we could win
If a Mom and Dad were in the home
Kids are raising themselves because
Mom is on crack and Dad is long gone

Our nation put its trust in money
Will buy anything anyone will sell
Every fallen nation stopped trusting God
Just before it fell

Nedra Anthony

The Lost Lamb

I tried my best to be good
But joy it did not bring
Until I learned about Jesus
Who is Savior, Lord and King

I have had some happy days
But in them was no peace
Since I met the Savior
My peace has been increased

Even the moutains that I face
Are much easier to climb
My point of view has changed
And it really blows my mind

My past no longer hinders me
Each day I flourish and grow
Things that had me bound
I am learning to let them go

Knowing that He loves me
I have stopped living in fear
I give all praise to Him
While I am still here

He is preparing me to live with Him
In a place not ruled by time
I am the lost lamb
Jesus the shepherd
Left the flock to find

Not A Failure

The Lord let me struggle
To the point of dispair
In my heart I knew
He was always there

One day, I just got weary
I had lost the will to fight
I thought my faith had failed me
But I was walking by sight

All the praying I had done
Prayed for hours every day
I knew that he was listening
He did not see it my way

By now, I was getting the message
I began learning to seek His plan
For when I first said I believed
I put my life into His hands

He is pressing out the wrinkles
He is removing every spot
Showing me with His love
A failure I am not

Nedra Anthony

The Difference

What is this difference
I feel inside of me
I am not the same
I have been set free

I ask Jesus to take over my life
To help me deal with my problems
I am in so much trouble
Only You can help me solve them

Help me put my fears behind me
Help me to make the right choice
Help me as I read Your word
To have an ear to hear Your voice

I need You to walk with me
Help me stop clinging to my past
Show me how to walk in Your love
I know it will forever last

I still have the same problems
With another point of view
I know there is a difference
Inside of me is something new

I have reached a turning point
I was afraid I never would
Bluer skies, greener grass
A long time since I felt this good

The Miracle

A different kind of peace is within
Now I know what I must do
Learn all about the difference
The difference Jesus is You

Without A Flaw

God is a God of goodness
He makes the sun shine bright
Along with the moon and stars
That shine all through the night

He is a merciful and mighty God
He made me a part of His team
He is the reason the sky is blue
The reason the grass is green

He made the mountains to line the sky
Made what we can and cannot see
The decision was already made
He created you and me

After all was said and done
He took the time to rest
Man decided to eat from the tree
Man failed his only test

He disobeyed what God had said
Man made his first wrong choice
Instead of listening to his Creator
He heeded another's voice

The heart of God was grieved
His plan was not for this to be
He showed His love for His creation
When He prepared another tree

The Miracle

One had to come to redeem man
At stake was your soul and mine
God stepped out of eternity
And stepped into time

God's love is purer than diamonds
The God no man ever saw
God who created the universe
Gave us spirits without a flaw

Nedra Anthony

You And Me

To keep us from trusting God
Or learning to follow His plan
The devil will do what he must
To destroy the souls of man

He has so many traps
We can get caught up in
Anything he throws your way
Will lead you into sin

His focus is on our children
Shooting killing and running wild
Many are abused or neglected
Having very little reason to smile

Some are living with parents
Father and Mother both on drugs
They learn to make it on their own
With very few kisses or hugs

Looking for love they go to gangs
All night the streets they roam
Not wanting to go to the place
That they must call their home

They have no respect for life
Think it is an honor to be crazy
And think it is an attribute
Stealing from others or being lazy

The Miracle

No self-worth drink and drugs
Have taken over our city
Nothing is being done about it
Everyone says what a pity

If they keep thinking they are nothing
Nothing they will continue to be
If a change is going to come
It must come through you and me

Nedra Anthony

Not One Step

There are times I stray away
From the path that God has set
Everytime I strayed away
I only found regret

It is after one of those times
I lacked the courage to confess my sin
Unbelief had me convinced
I could not help but do it again

The hard part when sin is confessed
Is for me to forgive myself
The only way to get back in step
Was to turn to Jesus for help

I always blamed someone else
But never did I blame me
I was trying to run game on God
By His spirit He helped me see

The reason Jesus gave His life
Was to give my life new meaning
He would teach how to live for Him
With every fiber of my being

I am closer to Him than yesterday
I will be closer if He gives me tomorrow
He has been with me all the time
Even in my pain and sorrow

The Miracle

He opened my eyes so I could see
I could not make it on my own
He promised He would be with me
Not one step would I take alone

Nedra Anthony

No Matter Where

The Lord is my Shepherd
My Savior and Master
Before I met Him
My life was a disaster

He shows me as I go
How to obey His will
Leads me to the waters
That are calm and still

To make it down life's roads
With Him and common sense
He let's me rest in meadows
He daily gives me strength

He knows I do not doubt
He is the Son of God
He gives me comfort
By His staff and His rod

My enemy can do nothing
He knows he is unable
He just stands and watches
As my Shepherd prepares my table

Death lurks in the shadows
Of the valleys that I walk
My Shepherd is always with me
While we walk we talk

The Miracle

He knows about the times
I am at my lowest low
His Goddness and mercy follow me
No matter where I go

Nedra Anthony

Your View

I must work out my salvation
Allowing Jesus to lead the way
As I search the word of God
I must take the time to pray

The Bible tells me how to walk
It will teach me how to stand
I understand it will not be easy
To learn to follow His command

Faith will lead me to the light
My doubts have kept me away
Old things are becoming new
Since I learned how to pray

In my weakness is His strength
He helps me to keep fighting back
The devil knows he rules no more
I am under constant attack

So I lift my eyes to the hills
To where my help comes from
The battle is His not mine
The work has all been done

Seeking God and His Kingdom
Will let His light shine through
He will change you from within
Then change your view of you

Not Cheap

The Lord does not accept me
For any good that I have done
It is because He loves me
Proved by the death of His Son

He gave His life on Calvary
He died for my salvation
Now He lives inside of me
I am a new creation

Jesus went to the grave
Took back the keys
After three nights and days
He was raised from death
With Him I was raised

I am grateful He chose me
So He could open my eyes
Had He not come when He did
I would not be alive

As I learn to walk in faith
I learn to put my pride aside
I learn to face my problems
I have stopped trying to hide

Now I can see more clearly
I am now rid of my dispair
He gives me courage to press on
I call His name He is there

I can remove mountains by faith
Does not matter how high or steep
Jesus paid the price salvation is free
But it was not cheap

The Miracle

He Was Sent

Thoughts are cities to conqueor
Mind renewed as you take control
Be led by the Holy Spirit
Do not be ruled by your soul

Keep your eyes on Jesus Christ
For you He shed His blood
He gave His life to save us
Because of His great love

The enemy cannot harm you if
The Holy Spirit leads your way
Each day you are given
Always take the time to pray

Daily grow in knowledge
To gain wisdom from God's word
Do not be ashamed to share it
With those who have not heard

Tell them of His unlimited love
About why His blood was shed
Tell them the good news
He rose from the dead

He came to save everyone
Who desired to repent
Tell them what He did for you
Is the reason He was sent

Nedra Anthony

My Level

When I got down on my knees
I knew just what I would say
I thought my perfect prayer
Would make God see it my way

But God made me look at the fact
Each time I confessed a sin
I had no intention of changing
I would confess that sin again

While kneeling there I realized
My words were filled with hate
The words I had spoken
Were not prayers, but a debate

He said any trial you go through
I will surely bring you out
I asked him to forgive me
To help me not to doubt

I started reading His word
I found the greatest treasure
He helped me to clearly see
He blessed me beyond measure

Desiring to walk in His will
Has turned my life around
Since I started walking with Him
I am reaching higher ground

The Miracle

Jesus is the light of my life
I am no longer condemned
He came down to my level
the only way I could to get to Him

Completed

I know the plan I have for you
God in Heaven has declared
I sent My Son to the cross
The way has been prepared

My plan is for your welfare
I do not make mistakes
Choose the path I have set
And you must walk by faith

Learn to obey my commands
Believe and trust My Son
Repent and confess your sins
There is still work to be done

Ask for what you need
Do not cease to pray
You have a determined enemy
He will try to block your way

He couldn't keep Me from giving you life
He wants to destroy the life I gave
That is why I sent My Son
Now your soul can be saved

Strive to have the mind of Christ
Knowing the enemy is defeated
I have begun a work in you
I will not stop until it's completed

The Miracle

Unspeakable Joy

Joy is knowing

Jesus loves me
For in Him I can be strong
I confess He forgives
If have done something wrong

Joy is

learning how to trust Him
Those times I am afraid
I learn to trust Him more
When I read what He said

Joy is knowing

When no words will come
His spirit will help me pray
He leads me down right paths
Helps me not want to go astray

Joy is knowing

He molds and shapes my life
Like a potter does with clay
He give me the ear to hear
When he has something to say

Nedra Anthony

Joy is knowing

Of His unchanging love
No one or nothing can destroy
When I gave my life to Jesus
He gave me unspeakable joy

The Miracle

Andrew

One day I asked my young neighbor
Do you like going to school
He answered,
I like going to school because
everybody thinks I am cool

I asked,
do you have a goal in mind
I have read how well you write
He answered,
It does not keep me warm
On a cold and rainy night

I knew how hard it was for him
I had known him all his life
I drove his mom to the hospital
After that I saw her twice

Andrew was smarter than his years
He paid the bills at the age of ten
A straight-A student selling drugs
I think of what might have been

I asked,
What about your mom and dad
Don't they care what you do
He answered,
They are my best customers
Do whatever I tell them to

Nedra Anthony

I am making a lot of money
As long as I don't get caught
And am I sharp or what
See the new clothes I bought

The next day
he was walking down the street
Someone did not think he was cool
From a car driving by he was shot
On his way to school

Mother's Love

When I was a little girl
I asked,
Mama, why do you love me
As she held me in her arms
After I fell out of a tree

She said,
You know when you hurt
I am hurting, too
Loving you through the pain
Is all I know to do

I said,
I know you love us all
What is your favorite's name
She said,
All of you are my favorite
I love you all the same

I asked,
How can you love us
All at the same time
She said,
God trusted me to give you life
All of you are mine

She added,
Now let's pray a little prayer
Ask for the pain to go away
I said,
Thank you, Lord, the pain is gone
Mama, can I go out and play

As I ran towards the door
I looked back to see her smile
Knowing my mother loved me
Made my life worthwhile

The Miracle

Too Much To Gain

Trusting in His promise
He would always be there
At the feet of Jesus
I laid my burdens and cares

I asked Him for His help
In my heart was a thirst
To do His will for my life
To seek His Kingdom first

He gave me living water
He invited me to drink
Everything changed that day
Even how I feel and think

Before I stopped drinking
I was filled to overflowing
I understood Him better
My faith just kept on growing

He guides me through each day
Teaching me I can be bold
He has given me assurance
It is well with my soul

With His cleansing blood
My sins have been erased
He loved me so much
He chose to take my place

Nedra Anthony

I give Him honor and I praise Him
He gave me the chance to choose
I chose to give my life to Him
I had too much to gain to lose

The Miracle

Worked Out

I had to finally put my life
Into God the Father's hand
It was the only way I could learn
To live according to His plan

Willful sin was running my life
I wanted to change destination
Then I was told by a friend
I could become a new creation

I was told it would not be easy
I had to stop walking by sight
Even if I stumbled and fell
I could learn to walk in the light

I started to resist temptation
Most times when it came around
Every time I ran after it
It ran me into the ground

I tried my best not to fail
Each time I did I would fall
I knew how much I needed him
But would hesitate to call

Then grief came out of nowhere
I had shed all of my tears
Jesus said just keep on pressing
And give Me all your fears

Nedra Anthony

I want you to walk in faith
That leaves no room for doubt
Believe in what I have said
I have already worked it out

The Miracle

Keep The Change

Mankind is uniquely made
Able to see and hear and talk
Man also has the ability
To feel and taste and walk

We can see the growth
Of a mighty tall oak tree
We hear birds singing sweetly
Or the roar of an angry sea

We can speak to each other
Sing praises to God above
We share our feelings with those
God gave us to love

We can taste the sweetness
Baked in Mama's apple pie
And the sweetness of God's grace
On whom we can rely

We can walk with our God
In the cool of the day
He gives us the privilege
In His name to pray

He even sent His Son
To die on Calvary
For Him it was certain death
So we could be made free

Nedra Anthony

He paid the ultimate price
Our destiny He rearranged
He paid more than enough
And told us to keep the change

The Miracle

Some Time

Sometimes when I have a moment
With a heart's desire to pray
I let a thought invade my mind
Then the desire fades away

Sometimes I get so busy
As I am hurrying on my way
I don't even take the time
To thank God for the day

Sometimes I have errands to run
Going from here to there
It doesn't even cross my mind
To go to God in prayer

Sometimes I get home just in time
To watch my favorite show
Instead of picking up my Bible
To allow my faith to grow

Sometimes I get so weary
Suffering with a hurting head
I finish my day I take a pill
Then go straight to bed

Sometimes when the storms came
Riding it out was not so smooth
I cried out to the Lord
Not one moment did I lose

I asked,
Why is all this happening, Lord
I am about to lose my mind
He said,
I waited so long to talk to you
I had to make you find some time

The Miracle

His Loving Care

God had a plan when He made man
He gave him total control
He gave him breath to breathe
Man became a living soul

He gave him power and authority
To rule over all creation
He gave him his own choice
Which led him to temptation

I fell into a lot of temptation
Doing what brought me misery
Knowing within my heart
What I sowed would return to me

On the day I realized
My life was in a mess
I knew I needed help
Not to mention I needed rest

He already knew I was coming
He knew just what I needed
All the trying I had done
Somehow, I never succeeded

But when Jesus came to live in me
On that day He lightened my load
He knew I finally understood
He paid the debt I owed

Nedra Anthony

I now make time every day
To go to Him in prayer
With every breath I am blessed
Walking in His loving care

All Other Kings

God has a purpose for me
It is not to live in strife
A path has been prepared for me
That leads to eternal life

I knew a change had to come
Or I would end up dead
Nobody had any faith in me
No one believed a word I said

I needed to turn my life around
Needed to change my circumstance
I am alive today because
I was given a second chance

The day I called on Jesus I found
He was the one I needed to follow
To look at me I looked fine
But on the inside I was hollow

I lived so long in the darkness
I had no idea that I was lost
Until I heard that Jesus died
For me on Calvary's cross

I believe He rose from the dead
He is no longer in the grave
I had found the only way
My soul could be saved

Nedra Anthony

Now He is a part of my life
I know the joy His love can bring
I am a child of the King
All other kings call King

The Miracle

His Grace

Jesus is my bridge over troubled water
Those times when I fall in
He gathers me in His loving arms
He forgives me again and again

I tried to walk the middle road
With one foot on each side
I discovered that did not work
No matter how hard I tried

He placed a thought in my mind
I let things stand in my way
I was my own worst enemy
I never took time to pray

I needed to be saved
Jesus saved me from myself
My back was against a wall
I knew only He could help

The fact that I want to serve Him
Is all that He requires
Now every day His blessings flow
Changing my heart's desires

Looking back I can clearly see
The reason Jesus had to come
To tell me that he loved me
In spite of the wrong I have done

Nedra Anthony

I am learning to trust him
He helps me run life's race
He protects me with His love
He surrounds me with His grace

The Miracle

Walk In His Will

God used peolple in my life
To help me realize
Jesus Christ went to the cross
Saving my soul was His prize

I was afraid and all alone
There was no one I could call
My life was going downhill
I had no one to break my fall

I had no idea which way to turn
I was afraid of how fearful I felt
My world came tumbling down
Not one person I knew could help

After I had reached my bottom
Thanking God I was still alive
I knew He had come for me
Or I never would have survived

I asked Jesus to come into my life
He immediately took control
He took away the fear I felt
Deep down in my soul

As His words flooded my mind
My thoughts were being transformed
Jesus has loved me all the time
Even before the day I was born

Nedra Anthony

Sometimes I can feel His presense
When my mind is quiet and still
He gives me the heart's desire
To learn to walk in His will

The Miracle

On My Knees

My soul cried out for freedom
My flesh tried to muffle the sound
Then Jesus came and set me free
He turned my life around

Until Jesus took control
Before I learned how to pray
Anything my mind could think
I would let it have its way

The world is losing its hold on me
Since all my sins I have confessed
I have let go of old things
That kept me living with stress

A new spirit is living within me
Daily I walk in victory
Learning there is a good side
To all of life's adversity

He guides me through life's valleys
When I cannot find words to say
Those times I step off the path
He helps me find my way

All power was given to Jesus
My enemy trembles when He sees
The same power rise up in me
When I get on my knees

In The End

God gave His word to inform us
We would be under constant attack
We trust Him no matter what
We know He has our back

Every test or trial we must face
Was nailed to Calvary's cross
He loved us even before
We knew that we were lost

Whatever we are going through
Body may be racked with pain
By His stripes we were healed
We will be well again

He is with us as we go through
Helps us deal with our distress
In weakness He gives us strength
Which will lead to our success

Put your life in His hands
His love is a reality
He works until we all are
The way He intended us to be

Before He returned to the Father
He left us this command
To ask to knock to seek to find
How we fit into His plan

The Miracle

He has given us His power
Which he expects us all to use
Trust in Him and you will find
In the end you cannot lose

Nedra Anthony

Useful Vessel

The Father knew His plan for me
As He laid the Earth's foundation
I would be one who would believe
I could become a new creation

He laid all of my sins on Jesus
Gave me the courage to overcome
He knew before the beginning
It was His will I wanted done

He allowed this circumstance
I had to call upon His name
From that day to this
I have never been the same

He lifted a veil from my eyes
Told me to leave my past behind
To put away all childish things
To let His word renew my mind

The Holy Spirit will help me seek
What God has planned for me
He will lead me to the truth
The truth will make me free

He will shape and mold my life
Any way that He might choose
He will turn me into a vessel
That He has plans to use

The Miracle

I Am

One day I asked the Lord
How come I am so weak
He said,
My child, read My word
It says you should be meek

If you let me work through
This lesson you will learn
Your sins must be left behind
From them all you must turn

I will supply your every need
I will put your life on track
Help you lay aside every weight
That has held you back

Only your spirit is born again
Not your body or your soul
Follow the path I have set
Stay on it to reach your goal

Know all that I have done
To show My love for you
Build on your measure of faith
You will know My word is true

The Father sent Me to save you
I was the sacrificial lamb
It is up to you to believe
I am who I said I am

Nedra Anthony

A New Song

To bring me my salvation
To show me real true love
God sent His Son to save me
From Heaven up above

He came, He died, He rose again
He willingly took my place
On the cross before He died
He revealed God's loving grace

He even gave me the privilege
To come to Him in prayer
Whenever I call on His name
He is always there

I want Him to use me
To bless a sister or brother
One of the commands he left us
To have love for one another

By letting His spirit be my guide
I am gaining the victory
Like you, I am locked in battle
Fighting who I used to be

His word renews my mind
It tells me to tell you
Of the many tests and trials
He has brought me through

The Miracle

Sharing has made a difference
I have pointed some souls to Him
After telling my story they knew
I was sinking and learned to swim

My faith grows as I learn
The joy His love can bring
I am putting old things behind me
Now a brand new song I sing

Nedra Anthony

Complete In Christ

Living life without God
Will not reveal the revelation
That Jesus died in our place
So we could receive salvation

The love of God covers everyone
In His heart is plenty of room
He loved us all even before
We entered our mother's womb

Much time is spent running from God
Many lives are filled with fear
Scared of death afraid to live
Of God did not want to hear

I was stuck in a losing battle
Did not have the courage to fight
I stayed at home all day long
Then ran the streets all night

But I was tired of running
There had to be another way
Before I even had the thought
I got on my knees to pray

I confessed all that came to mind
Every sin and fear and doubt
I knew that only God
Could help me work it out

The Miracle

Trusting Him takes practice
I must learn to tame my soul
The more I learn the eaiser it gets
To give Him total control

So when there is a battle to fight
I will not go down in defeat
Because in my heart I know
In Christ I am complete

www.ingramcontent.com/pod-product-compliance
Lightning Source LLC
Chambersburg PA
CBHW030711110426
R18122000001B/R181220PG42736CBX00007B/9